Behind the Artist's Eyes

By Violet Snook

D0910894

UltraViolet Publishing

First published in the USA by
UltraViolet Publishing 2012

Copyright ©2012 Violet Snook
All rights reserved.

ISBN: 0615612121

ISBN 13: 978-0615612126

Printed and bound in the USA by CreateSpace

Permission was granted for use of all pictures
and actual names used in this book.

Dedication

I dedicate this book to my family and friends who have supported me through the splatters of paint and the ongoing strokes of the brush: the unpredictable designs and colors that make up my life.

"This book is full of life that shouldn't be hidden away on a dusty shelf. Once you finish reading it, please pass it on to someone else." – L. C. G.

Intro

If your life is a movie, which I believe it is, then at every different part there is a new song to sing, a song that tells that part of your life and brings you closer to who you really are. Songs are always changing throughout the new sets, new lighting, new characters brought into your life, and the developing new you. For every life that is brought into this world another script is written, beyond the cracks of your imagination, somewhere far back beyond your consciousness. And for every soul brought into this world, a new gift has been given. A new challenge has been accepted. And so, as I tell you my story I will introduce songs that convey that part of my life, songs that resonate with me.

Also, I want you to remember the story is never complete and the movie is never ending. Despite where I stop, my life continues beyond the conscious mind.

Chapter 1

Sleep Baby Sleep
By Rachel Rambach

Sleep baby sleep, thy father tends the sheep, thy mother shakes the dreamland tree and down fall pleasant dreams for thee, sleep baby sleep…

The Start

A new life was born on March 7th, 1992, and I was that child. A new star was burning bright somewhere in the sky that night. For with every new soul that is brought into this world a new star is born. I came out "screaming mad" as they say. With all the commotion, bright lights, and cold air hitting my warm skin, how could I be happy? But I was one healthy baby and that's what mattered most. Right? Yes. I was an answer to prayer, lots of prayer! I became a "Cling-on" my parents say — a little girl who couldn't let go of her mother, or father for that matter. God had brought me into this world, and only God knew I was the perfect one for them.

But at only sixteen months old, something would happen that would change my life forever.

That hot July day of 1993, my mom remembers well. She was cutting the grass, with me in a backpack. That's when it happened. I had made a strange sound, alarming Mom. She stopped the lawnmower, and ran inside to see what was wrong. She called for my dad who quickly came from wherever he was in the house. My head was slumped over, no breathing could be detected. After I recovered my parents called first the family doctor, and then the closest hospital and they told my parents to bring me right down.

What really had happened? I had my first seizure. God has given me a gift that no one realized until that day. That gift is epilepsy. Truthfully, no one recognized it as epilepsy until a few years later when the pattern of seizing didn't stop. But from that point on, they (meaning doctors, neurologists, and, of course, my parents) tried to "fix it," "remodel me," so I didn't have to deal with it, so I could have an "ordinary" or "normal" or "average" childhood, whatever that means. I didn't have that, of course. God didn't want me to have that, but I didn't know that God had other plans for me. I was only a child.

Chapter 2

The Wonderful Thing About Tiggers
By Richard M. Sherman
&
Robert B. Sherman

The wonderful thing about Tiggers, is Tiggers are wonderful things. Their tops are made out of rubber. Their bottoms are made out of springs. They're bouncy, trouncy, flouncy, pouncy, fun, fun, fun, fun, FUN! But the most wonderful thing about Tiggers, is I'm the only one...

I'm Different

So God has given me this gift, this wonder, this challenge. That is what my parents told me. That was their explanation for why I had this disorder, this challenge. As a little girl, the explanation suited me. It is certainly better then "possessed by demons" even if I didn't know that expression at the time. But they, themselves, didn't know what they were doing. For like the doctors and neurologists, they, too, wanted it gone. They wanted to crumple up the gift and throw it in the trash. They wanted me to be able to do things like the other kids could. They wanted me to have an "ordinary" or "normal" life? Riii-ght. **So** not me. I'm naturally different, but I was only a little girl and all I saw was that they were trying to help, and help was appreciated. To be honest, I didn't want the "gift" either at the time. I didn't like being slower than my peers, and not being able to go onto the monkey bars. The way I saw it, epilepsy was a bother; it held me back, took away my freedom and prevented me from being able to do some of the things I wanted to do. It just wasn't right. I was different, and yet I wanted to be "normal". That was not going to happen of course, but I always had my hopes.

Chapter 3

Potter's Wheel
By John Denver

Take a little clay, put it on a wheel, get a little hint how God must feel. Give a little turn, listen to it spin, make it in the shape you want it in. Earth and water and wind conspire. With human hands, and love, and fire…

Human Hands

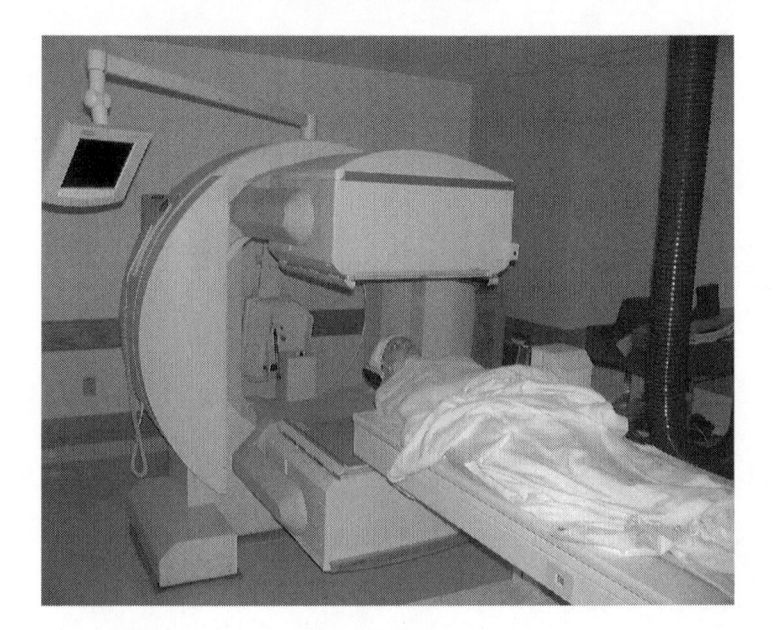

Figure 1 - Me in SPECT Scanner

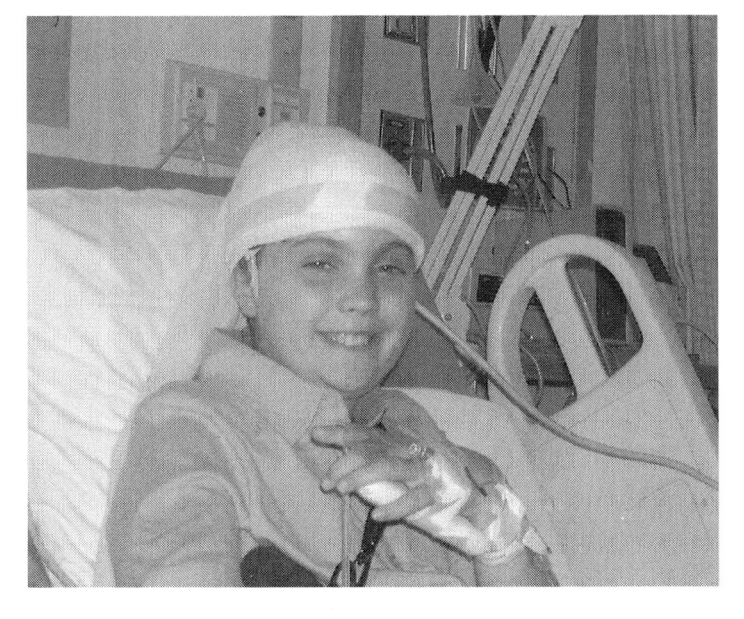

Figure 2 - Me, with IV in hand, and 24/7 EEG
headgear

Epilepsy seemed to take up my whole life. If I
wasn't at school, I was most likely in the hospital
for another "remodeling" of sorts. I grew up
having an extensive vocabulary. Starting at a
young age, I knew some pretty big words that my
peers and many older people to this day have
never heard. They are words that came with the
territory of going back and forth to the hospital
for various procedures revolving around my
epilepsy, such as EEG, neurological, SPECT
scan, and MRI.

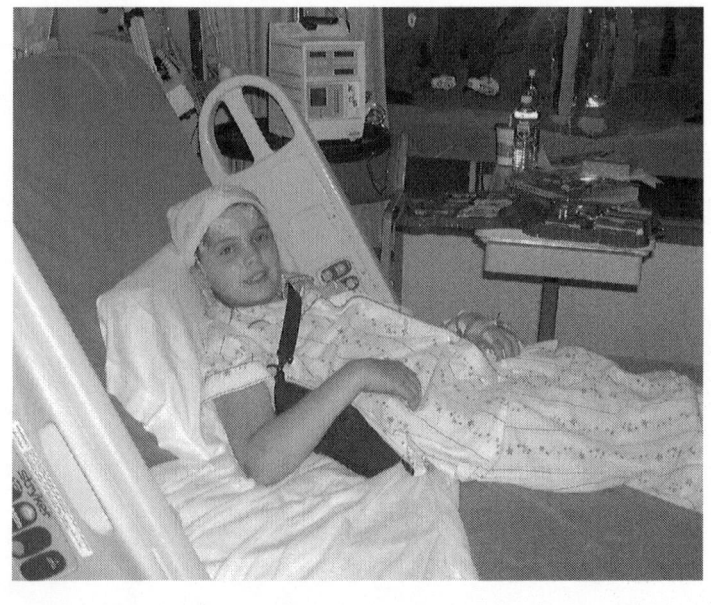

Figure 3 - Yep, still here! With cable, met neighbor

The human hands like to make everything better. They like to make everything good, and that's exactly what the doctors, neurologists, and my parents were trying to do. They wanted to "fix me up", make me better, as if I were sick, and "model" me to their liking, the outside world's liking. In short, as I see it now, they were trying to resculpt me to be the "perfect average individual". Yeah, right! There's no such thing, but it doesn't mean they couldn't try. I couldn't try. As I said before, it's not like I wanted to be different.

Chapter 4

> ## More Than Useless
> ### By Relient K
>
> Sometimes I think that I'm not any good at all. And sometimes I wonder why, why I'm even here at all. But then, you assure me. I'm a little more than useless. And when I think I can't do this, you promise me that I'll get through this and do something right. Do something right for once…

Social Life

Aside from "dealing" with my epilepsy, my social life wasn't exactly typical. I was no social butterfly. I was shy and insecure. I didn't approach my peers. I let them come to me, and most often they didn't. I look back now and say God had His reasons. If God has a plan for my life then He has His reasons for who He puts and doesn't put before me for friends. Besides, it's not like nobody knew me. Growing up in the

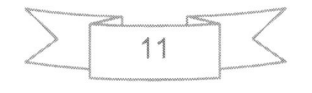

small town of Meredith, it's hard not to be known.

A good example of this was Girl Scouts. One of my peers introduced me to it, and soon I was sucked in, thanks to Girl Scout leader, Lucy. When I began, the troop was overwhelmingly large. I first felt like I didn't belong, so insecure and shy I shrunk back from the crowd, keeping quite. All the girls had their "clicks" and I was the newcomer, the one that didn't quit fit in…yet.

Girl Scouts did help me branch out into the community with projects and, of course, cookies! Maybe that's the best way to meet your neighbors. I don't know, but that's how we did it. Mom and I would go around from house to house selling Girl Scout cookies. Most of our neighbors bought at least one box.

So the closest friend I had was a girl I shall call Karen, whom I met in first grade. In school, we were best buddies, Karen and I. But outside of school things would change. It was hard to get together. I probably went over to her house once and she over to mine, but that was about it. We lost connection after that year and I was once again on my own.

That said, I didn't have any more really "close" friends until third grade. A girl whom I shall call Crystal had just moved here and didn't have any friends yet. I was curious and so I decided to try to get to know her. We hit it off, I guess. Looking back now, I don't know how we did it. We were exact opposites.

It seems that from that point on I had some sort of knack for getting to know the new kids on the block, those who seemed to get "discluded" from the rest of my peers, those who were different in one way or another and didn't quite fit in. Truthfully, I was open. I still am. I didn't and still don't "disclude" anyone based on race, color, sex, or interest. I respect people's differences and opinions. I've come to be compassionate and understanding. I was kind and respected all my peers and they returned the favor. I certainly wasn't the popular kid, and often didn't make friends with every new kid, but I did my best to reach out to those who I could see weren't included. My peers accepted me, and that's really all that mattered. I didn't get picked on, and often, to my eyes, it seemed as if some of them feared me, not knowing what I might do, or how I might react. It was as if they didn't really know me well enough to think otherwise.

Despite how it might sound, I only had a handful of friends throughout my childhood. Some of them came and went while others stayed longer. But, still, they too were only there for a season. I am careful and cautious when making friends. I intentionally don't rush through it. Usually my friends find out about my epilepsy. It's whether they can accept that fact or not that determines whether the friendship will last. I like to be direct, but typically I don't bring it up until something happens that I have no other obvious choice but to tell the truth. I couldn't do things like the other kids. For example, I couldn't stay up late and I had to monitor and take medicine everyday for my seizures. This in itself definitely influenced my friendships and my overall social life.

Chapter 5

On my Way
By Phil Collins
'Cause I'm on my way now - well and truly. I'm on my way now…

The Incident

In third grade <u>Brother Bear</u> had just come out. One of the songs in the movie was <u>On my Way</u> by Phil Collins, which was a hit favorite of mine. I think it was for Crystal, too. Both of us would be swinging on the swings and singing that song. They were good times! God had put this newfound wonderful friend in my life. Despite the significant amount of differences we had, we still had some similarities such as that, singing on the swings during recess.

Recess was a time for relaxation and play. The "playing with another" was something I was not familiar with until that year. I had spent many recesses before relaxing and spending quality time with myself and God, because I didn't have friends. Now, obviously, I don't believe I knew it was God who I spent time with at that point in my life. God certainly meant something different to me at that point in my life than He does now. I don't remember how I thought of Him back then, but my intuition tells me it was indeed different.

On one overcast early November day in 2002, I was hanging out with Crystal as I typically did at recess, when suddenly things shifted. The black colorless trees came to life, staring back at me. I saw wild animals and creatures shaped within the trees, leaping out at me. The air started to visually waver. Fear plummeted through me. An aura had set on, and for those reading who don't know, an aura is a pre-seizure warning – something that occurs before a major seizure takes place. This is often described as a sensation, visual or emotional, or even just a feeling. Obviously, for me it was a visual sensation – "Wild Eyes," right in line with an emotional sensation – fear. I named this aura "Wild Eyes" for truly that's what it obviously felt like. My eyes were playing tricks on me, and I knew it, but there was nothing I could do to stop it. Knowledge and intuition took over. I excused myself from play (something I think I must have done often) and went to find the nearest playground teacher.

Unfortunately, the playground teacher I found was not one I had gotten good vibes from before. She was a younger teacher with short cut brunette hair and a lean body. I had tried numerous times to ignore her and find a different playground teacher to go to. Today was not my lucky day. There was no other playground teacher close enough by that I could go to instead. I'd have to face this teacher now. I needed to get down to the nurse. Or so I thought.

"Excuse me," I must of said, "may I go down to the nurse?"

"Why do you need to go down to the nurse?" She asked me.

Hoping a simple answer would suffice I said, "I'm having Wild Eyes."

"What's that?" She asked, obviously not educated about my needs.

Great! I thought, starting to get antsy. I explained the best I could, "It's where my eyes see shapes within the trees of wild creatures.

And the trees are staring at me angrily. I'm going to have a seizure if I don't go down to the nurse."

"What's a seizure?" was her next question, completely oblivious to my vibes of frustration, fear, and growing anxiety.

By now I'm irritated, but I take a deep breath and once again begin to explain to the best of my ability. "A seizure is caused by the electrical signals in my brain..." I didn't get to complete my definition for a seizure, because in that very moment I demonstrated it. Hint, hint.

As I've heard it, the playground teacher panicked. Full of fear, she radioed down to the nurse's office, who responded within seconds. The nurse raced up the hill to the "Older Kids Playground" with wheelchair in hand. (I want to make clear that this part I've pieced together from various bits and pieces I overheard.)

I awoke to a slightly blurred vision of green grass surrounding my head and the nurse's gentle voice somewhere in the background before closing my eyes once again, falling gracefully into a second seizure.

I do not know the specifics of the seizures that happened that day, but most likely, drawing from past knowledge, I had stopped breathing and my body went limp. Back in those days my full-blown seizures could cause quite a scare to all involved.

As I awoke from the second seizure, I sat up and came to. I'm pretty confidant the nurse reached out her hand to me, and I accepted it gratefully. I stood up, and as I did, the nurse said, "I'd like you to get in the wheelchair in case you have any more seizures on the way down the hill." Having no other choice that my brain could at that point comprehend, I accepted and sat down in the wheelchair. On the way down the hill, heads turned to look at me, and the whispers of "What happened?" "Is she going to be OK?" filled the air. I was completely embarrassed. I hated that feeling, even to this day.

I'm fairly certain that once in the nurse's office, the nurse called my parents. My mom then came and picked me up. Full-blown seizures were not taken lightly.

I would not forget that naive playground teacher, nor the event that occurred. However, I do believe now that God had a good intention when He kept me stuck there. Looking back, I didn't have enough time to safely make it down to the nurse's office alone. God knew that, I didn't. He kept me there to keep me safe. Even though it didn't seem like it then.

The incident did change the playground teachers role and what they needed to know. I'm pretty confident that the year after that recess incident, all playground teachers knew the kids individual needs, those who had epilepsy and those who might need other kinds of assistance. And most importantly, all knew what epilepsy was and the appropriate actions to take.

I was definitely glad that my incident had changed the way the school looked at a playground teacher's role. Though, like any third grader would be, I was a little disappointed that it had to be **my** event that had pushed them to do something about it. I had never had anything happen nearly as severe after that.

At this time, brain surgery was discussed and dismissed, for the risks were too high and the help to slim. There was almost a guarantee I would have lost half my visual field. There was also a good possibility that I would have had to relearn many skills, like speaking and reading. And the biggest risk of all was that I might die to brain infection during the week that my scull would remain open for the surgery. My parents prayed and prayed, and God directed them down a different road.

Chapter 6

Believe in Myself
By Karen Brake

Gotta keep going, everything is a brand new challenge for me. I will believe in myself, this is the only start for me...

Technology to the Rescue

God works in mysterious ways, sometimes without our knowing it. He put down a new and different path for us to follow: A path of the new, the unheard of, the path of neurofeedback – a biofeedback for the brain. This new system literally retrains the brain by picking up brainwave (EEG) signals, filtering them, and providing the feedback which allows the brain to learn new ways of functioning.

Dad had heard of neurofeedback and had begun learning about it before we, as a family, started to explore it as a possible way of taming my seizures. My neurologist was skeptical about how much neurofeedback might help, but didn't discourage us from trying it before the possibility of brain surgery.

God opened new doors and windows. He showered Dad with many different training sessions to attend and varied professional opinions. Some of these Mom and I attended in various states, including California and Massachusetts. As God would have it, practitioners to whom Dad spoke in this newly developing field believed that it could work! Hope was in the air, and the Snook family ventured on.

God had His hand in this all the way through. Dad sent off an email to three different top professionals describing my situation. Miraculously, two of them got back to him right away. One of them introduced us to a doctor in western Massachusetts, who got in touch with Dad immediately. After talking over the phone, the doctor helped Dad get into a professional training class which had been scheduled for the very next weekend! Wow! Now that's fast. Initial appointments were scheduled immediately after, like the up-coming Monday.

In May, 2003, Dad started training my brain with our first neurofeedback system called EEG Spectrum, one that uses brainwaves to control a game, such as moving a spacecraft forward. After doing daily sessions with me for several months, Mom and Dad began to see small improvements and so continued on. For me, it was entertaining and fun, but I didn't get the point of it, not that I can recall, anyway.

Throughout the months and years, God blessed us with a total of three systems, each of which was an improvement on the last, but still not the best. Dad was encouraged by the brief response in my brainwaves that he saw during a trial run offered by the creator of the LENS system. He saw potential. So Mom and Dad both took training and bought a LENS system that could be used at home. Dad asked the system's creator if he could help in any way. The offer was appreciated and so began a close working relationship.

As issues arose with regard to the system, Dad's best skills were put to work. Having spent most of his career as a fantastic computer engineer, Dad began working to improve on the Lens protocol. He learned a lot about how the system worked and how it interacted with the brainwaves. The creator encouraged Dad to present his findings at a conference on the LENS system. Dad took him up on the offer. Eventually, confusion and chaos erupted and Dad's hard work on the system was set aside by the creator, for a concern about his business.

Continually determined, Dad pressed on, and in time, he invented his own system he called Neuro-Gen. Now **this** was good. No, not good, great! Fantastic. Amazing. Absolutely perfect. Yes, I do in fact mean perfect. No bugs, no flaws, completely perfect. And I flourished, improving in leaps and bounds. I could focus easier and think quicker.

Overall, my reading comprehension scores, once way below average, had significantly improved over time, while my seizures completely stopped!! Yes, my seizures did in fact stop!

Dad was so encouraged and fascinated with neurofeedback that soon enough, it became his new career focus, and a new company was being built. That company is called Mind-Brain Training Institute. Entrepreneurial dad strikes again!

Naturally, starting a new business is neither quick nor easy. Money became tight. While finances started to waver, Dad pressed onward feeling moved by God and the Holy Spirit to reach out and help other adolescences and young adults who were struggling just to stay afloat in the world. This was his mission, his real goal.

The Mind-Brain Training Institute still stands today, striving to make a difference in individuals' lives. I'm sure that many clients Dad has helped through the years will say that he is a hero in the greatest way. I know Dad is for me, and he always will be that hero who saved me from brain surgery and showed me, along side God, the way out of the darkness and into the light.

Chapter 7

Daddy's Little Girl
By Jesse McCartney
You just turned eighteen a week ago, and you want to learn what you don't know. You're grown up, don't need permission, find out what you've been missing…

Growing Up

As a tween going into my teen years, I got to taste freedom for the first time. Since 2003, I had been seizure free! In fact I had nearly lost all consciousness of my epilepsy. I had been doing Neurofeedback and a combination of two medications, which seemed to have controlled it. Success! At least, from the human standpoint. Finally, human hands were controlling the gift I was given.

Going into middle school (which was connected to the high school by a separate wing) I had nothing to fear. I wasn't active in seizing. In fact, the way I like to think about it is like a volcano that can erupt at anytime, an active volcano can change and be dormant and not erupt. I was like the dormant volcano. I could not erupt, could not seize. Therefore the nurse's office was almost like a foreign place to me, and if I could avoid it, I would.

God gave me a chance to see another side of things, gave me a chance to do things I otherwise would not have had the opportunity to do. He gave me a chance to grow, to blossom in more ways than one. God showed me another part of me I had no idea about as I watched the movie The Incredibles.

The movie opened up a new road, another side of me of which I had been unaware. I was always an artist, but never a writer. I was a horrible speller and therefore didn't like to write. I was slow, but precise and neat with my letters, and unfortunately, that wasn't good. I had a scribe for most of my classes to take notes and for lengthy assignments.

The Incredibles changed that right around, unlocking my imagination to another world where numerous stories and adventures awaited me. I found that movies would form in my mind easily and naturally. It was as though I were the playwright and the director. Naturally, I starred in quite a few of them. It was the character Violet Parr who showed me the wonderful ways I could heal through storytelling. Through her I found ways to solve my current conflicts and problems at hand, and I found peace and comfort along with satisfaction in the notion of her presense. I loved my imagination from sixth grade on, and loved to write. Daddy's little girl was growing confidant.

For me, writing was a secret formula that I never knew about before <u>The Incredibles</u> showed me where it was and how to use it. The family of supers guided me through this process in a story, which felt more like an adventure to me.

This is why: In order to write a story, I would first let it become a movie in my mind. When I had it just right, I would sit and copy down the dialog from my mind. That was my story. That's all that there is to it, folks.

Writing was only one of the many things that changed for me. Writing was just the start of a building confidence inside me. I had an opportunity to learn how to drive when I was sixteen. Having been seizure free, I would have qualified to get my license. Dad wanted me to work on my hand eye coordination before I did. Like all things, that took time, and time I felt I didn't have. So daddy's little girl took matters into her own hands. I gave up practicing. In addition, I didn't have a really good motivation to get my license. Transportation was always easy. But it certainly made me feel awkward when most of my peers were getting their licenses.

God presented me with another opportunity to grow even more. In 2007, our Girl Scout troop was invited to a Girl Scout Jamboree out in Minnesota at the St. Olaf Collage campus. By this point the troop had shrunk dramatically, and was now pretty small. I was still very much the lone ranger of the group, but had at least connected with one of the girls. All of us were excited about the prospect of going. My mom, on the other hand, was less than convinced. She was concerned for my safety, for she had never let me go anywhere outside of the state by myself. The solution? She joined as a Girl Scout leader. Daddy's little girl was growing in confidence and much more.

Chapter 8

Breakaway
By Kelly Carkson

I'll spread my wings and I'll learn how to
fly. I'll do what it takes till I touch the sky…

Learning to Fly

I can't deny that the trip to Minnesota was
spiritual, because it was in many ways. In fact, it
was an opportunity to rely on God. To draw Him
near and remind me that I am not alone even
when it appears that I am.

As our troop made our way through the airports
and security, we found ourselves in a new terrain.
We stayed in a tight-knit group, per Girl Scout
Safety wise requirements, until we got to the
dorms of the St. Olaf college campus. We took
time for unwinding before hitting the campus
grounds. The evening was filled with an
introduction to Jamboree life and meeting up
with the other participating troops from across
the country. The opening ceremony was
exciting, musical, and overwhelming for all of us.

Just imagine a football field packed with Girl Scouts in uniform, all singing Girl Scouts Together. Yes, my mom was there, but in reality she wasn't. She kept her distance, but was there for when I really needed her. You see, Girl Scout leaders lead by challenging the girls to take the lead. Good-bye, Mom! This was just the start and only day one. I would soon, for the first time ever, be "on my own."

God was very good to me even when I wasn't looking. He provided me with a foundation to fly. I found myself navigating the campus alone half of the time, the other half I had friends with me, girls from my troop. This was huge, I don't even know how many girls were there, but I do know we filled the campus dorms. To my surprise, I was calm. I didn't panic. I used maps, both mental and physical. I also looked and asked for directions when I was lost. I remember the toughest thing to do was keeping track of the time. It would go by so fast.

During this trip, Kira, one of the girls from our troop that I felt the closest too, became closer to me and I drew closer to her. We weren't buddies yet, but we did begin to see each other in a new light. I was showing a different side of me that I had hid for a long time and I was becoming more visible. I saw a more gentle side to her, something I hadn't noticed before.

Along the way, we also spent time at the Mall of America! This mall was gigantic! Four floors, all filled with shops. Here I started developing my own taste for clothing. The diva in me came out to shine and play. Being lean, I had a tendency to look at the more form-fitting shirts, than the more commonly lose fitting T's, which I had been wearing up until this point. I hadn't really had a style before, so for me this was only the beginning.

By the end of our trip, independence was setting in and my beautiful wings were starting to grow. However, unlike the other girls, I still couldn't stay up late, and another crook in the road, a twist of fate, would tear one of my delicate wings I was so eagerly trying to grow.

Chapter 9

Angels
By Within Temptation

Blinded by faith, I couldn't hear, all the whispers, the warnings so clear...

Fallen angel, tell me why? What is the reason, the thorn in your eye?...

A Flash Back to The Past

In the summer of 2009 I was well on my way to being off all medication and only doing Neurofeedback to continue being seizure free! The excitement was almost overwhelming. Could I truly go off all medication and continue to have zero seizures? Only in my wildest dreams had I ever thought it was possible, and yet, now, in that moment, I was just days away from finding out.

Well, to drown out the excitement, God had taken another child of His, another family member of ours, home again to Heaven. The earthly devastating sorrow overtook my entire family. I, however, having barely known our family member, felt little pain, at least, that I was aware of anyway. Needless to say, a trip was planned to go out to Michigan for the funeral.

The road trip involved going through Canada. It sounded like fun! Or at least at first it did. I suddenly felt more and more down as the days got closer to the trip. Closer to going off all medication! But the rest of my family had lost that fact, too caught up in the earthly sorrow to remember. Or so that's what I had thought until my mom came up to me and asked, "What's the matter?"

I told her. She figured out a way to celebrate and that involved getting my first and very own laptop! That cheered me up a bit. It was on sale at Wal-Mart, so I got a really good buy.

We had to get the laptop in the morning, because that's when the sale began. So it was a hectic morning and a crazy long day on the road. Off all medication for the first time, I was excited and nervous.

As the day got later and the night got longer, I started to get concerned when I couldn't fall asleep and it was well after eleven thirty at night. *Great*, I thought, *I'm bound to have a seizure at this rate. "No, no, you'll be okay." Please God let me not have a seizure tonight. Please Lord, please.* The suitcases were piled high behind my seat, so there was no way I could lean back far enough to get comfortable.

Once I got to sleep my worst fear came to life. I DID have a seizure. I made a strange sound which alerted my mom to the fact that something wasn't right. Now, by this point, no one knows how long I've already been seizing (though it's thought that the strange noise marked the start). Dad pulls the car over. I'm shaking, and gasping for breath, scaring Mom. Panicked, Mom calls 911, while Dad, more relaxed, administered a Lorazepam as well as a medicine called Diastat to stop the seizing.

Now, you would have thought that my parents would have reacted with less alarm, but truthfully, this seizure was a seizure like no other, and I hadn't had a seizure in literally years. This truly was, for my parents at least, a flash back to the past. My past.

By the time I had awakened, an ambulance had arrived. We were in Canada at this point. It was my first and, with any luck, my last ride in an ambulance. Though, for whatever reason I still can't quite understand, it felt like routine: the bright lights, the IV they put into my hand...

Once at the hospital, they did a check over to make sure I was all right. Although I was fine, the way I managed to do some of the things they were asking me to do was, looking back now, a bit strange. I got through, though, and that's all that mattered.

Needless to say, I was back on medication that night, but only on one of them, not on both. Thank you God! And, unannounced to me, I had months of freedom from seizures to look forward to, after this trip was over.

While the wings may have been freshly ripped, they were already on their way to mending.

Chapter 10

I'm in a Hurry
By Alabama

I'm in a hurry to get things done, don't know why. Rushing, rushing to last no more. All I really got a do is live and die, but I'm in a hurry and don't know why. Don't know why, I have to drive so fast my car has nothing to prove...

Independence is Key

To me, the entire world emphasizes independence and my teachers were no exception. They got on my case, alright. They didn't think I was independent enough for my age. They believed Mom and Dad needed to back off. I needed to get my driver's license and start doing things for myself, begin making my own decisions without their intervention.

It seems to me, that in the USA, independence is defined by the ability to live on your own without aid or help from others. It is emphasized from the very moment you step into high school. In New Hampshire, teenagers especially are encouraged to get their driver's license at sixteen years of age.

New Hampshire is a state where the countryside is prevalent and where every season changes with stunning color and temperature. To go to any big stores you have to be able to drive. Unless you are able to afford a taxi, which I believe is ridiculously expensive for the distance driven, you are out of luck.

To live on the back roads, like I do, makes it even more difficult if you can't drive. You aren't in walking distance of town, you don't have that option. It's not that I was stuck, but rather I couldn't go anywhere I wanted to without asking Mom or Dad for a ride. They were both very generous about their time and saying "Yes" to my requests. However, I will say, it's not the same as if I lived down town and were able to walk to the post office, library, or even just to the town docks and glace out at the water. Nobody I know knows how much of a luxury it is living in town.

However, at that point in my life, independence was not my main focus – getting through school was. Now, of course, that didn't stop teachers and friends from encouraging me to become more independent, to speak for myself, cook for myself, you know, the basics you have to be able to do in order to live on your own.

One of my friends was going through a similar struggle. She and I could relate and sympathize with each other. We were a support system for each other. My parents backed me up. As my parents were fond of pointing out, the teachers encouraging us didn't live with us. They weren't there twenty-four/seven watching us and seeing our struggles and weaknesses. They didn't know what was going on behind the scenes.

I'm not saying I didn't grow more independent, nor am I saying I didn't understand the importance of independence in my world. I did, and I still do. Independence is very much key to success. However, to the outside world's standards, I wasn't growing independent fast enough. I was growing independent at a slow and steady pace, which seemingly wasn't acceptable. I had to mature faster! "Faster, faster!" the world seemed to scream. But I couldn't mature any faster than at the pace I was going. I mean, come on! We're not all the same!

Let's face it, we're all different, and no one matures at the same pace. If we're all children of God, which I believe, then we are all made differently, and each one of us is individually independent enough for our age. However, I do understand that's not the world's view, and in the USA I'm not sure that it ever will be. But who cares? Uh—everybody. Yeah, right. I'm not sure I do…

Chapter 11

Supergirl
By Krystal Harris
I'm Supergirl! And I'm here to save the world, and I wanna know...who's gonna save me?...

The Super Inside Me

The Incredibles truly did inspire me. The character who influenced me the most was Violet Parr, the teenage daughter. I could readily identify with her, on some level I couldn't yet fully appreciate, I wanted very much to experience the kind of transition and growth that she experienced through her adventures. She soon became my idol. I grew from her. I found insight into myself by watching her.

Violet Parr grew into my spiritual guide. It was as though I could communicate with her internally. I found comfort in the notion that she was there, standing beside me. She was the understanding friend I never felt I had, the friend who could see where I was coming from and acknowledge me as I was. I would say we were two nearly identical people. Character and human. I sometimes thought she was the super within me. It sometimes felt as if she were prowling underneath my skin, a kind of alter ego.

It was eighth grade when I came to the realization that I wanted to change my name from Anna to Violet. Then it seemed to me that a lot of people were pronouncing my name "Ah - na" instead of "Ann – a". That was most likely because two other girls in my school pronounced their names that way. I didn't want to be confused with them. My reasons or "rationales" at the time were not sufficient. However, I was persistent. I didn't give up. I kept the idea going in my mind, formulating.

Finally, at age eighteen, I legally changed my name from Anna to Violet. That day I transformed internally. I saw and felt Violet becoming one with me. As a result, I felt a boost of confidence and I grew more independent in a year than anyone imagined I would. She was me. I was her – a Super. She had truly been the Super inside of me, who unfolded through me. I had begun to assume the confidence that I saw develop within her.

This transformation changed the way I looked, how I thought, and how I reacted to different situations. I was virtually a new person, very independent and expressive. My new clothing reflected my artistic motif, looking both stylish and artsy. I had begun to feel more like a young adult. I felt strong enough and open enough to reach out for help when I needed it. I was voted "most changed" girl in my senior class.

At Baccalaureate, I was the first up to perform, singing solo a version of <u>This is The Day</u>. I shocked my peers to silence, before the round of applause was given. Many complimented me afterwards in amazement.

Had I not transformed I would have never had the prom date I did. He came all the way up from Sarasota, Florida, just for the prom. I once again blew away my peers with such a magnificent date. I had all the girls wondering, "Who is that guy? And how did Violet catch him?"

I was so confident that I believed I could put epilepsy and my past behind me. I was growing new, more beautiful, wings. The road ahead, however, would not turn out nearly as smooth as I imagined. There were many bumps, rocks, and cracks before the end of Senior year that I would stumble through.

Chapter 12

Stand in the Rain
By Superchick

So stand in the rain. Stand your ground.
Stand up when it's all crashing down. You
stand through the pain. You won't drown,
and one day what's lost can be found. You
stand in the rain...

Reminder

God couldn't just let me slip into a new skin without reminding me of who I was. Fairly soon after I changed my name I started seizing. Not badly, just a few times. I didn't think much about it at the time, for there seemed to be explanations for each of them. For instance, I had one in a quiet Chinese restaurant at noon, but I had forgotten to take my morning meds so it only made sense that I suddenly had a seizure there.

I think God decided to jar me awake with a seizure in the produce section of the supermarket at the end of the first week of senior year of high school. Oh joy. I remember it well. I awoke to a crowd surrounding me. I felt stripped of the confidence I had gained throughout the years, and which had been boosted through the name change. It felt as though the new wings I believed I was growing had been torn from my body. Suddenly, I was feeling very vulnerable.

You see, my seizures weren't absence seizures, or even partials. They were tonic-clonics. I'd go unconscious, and lose practically all muscle tone. I might clench, or move my eyes strangely, or even make strange sounds, generally referred to as distress sounds or "baby noises". In rare cases, I would shake. You might be asking why I know all this. Well, truthfully, I don't know all of this because I don't remember. I ask questions of those who are with me, typically my mom or dad. I learn, and am still learning. What I have said is what they have relayed to me from their observations.

I had to gain back what I had lost in that experience. That wasn't easy. On top of that, my social structure took a downhill turn and so did my health. Was God testing me?

Chapter 13

Invisible
By Marie Digby

But the others, they couldn't seem to get past all the things that mismatched on the surface. And she would close her eyes when they laughed and she fell down the stairs. And the more that they joked and the more that they screamed, she retreated to where she is now. And she'll sing, take a little look at the life of Miss Always Invisible…

A Downhill Swing

It was only a week or two after that event in the supermarket that I was diagnosed with Lyme disease. The prognosis dramatically changed my mood and my mind. A scene from The Incredibles repeated itself as I rode home with my dad in the car from the doctor's appointment. The scene went like this: The plane has just exploded and Violet, Dash, and Mrs. Incredible are freefalling down to the ocean, the kids screaming. After hitting the water Dash starts to scream, "We're dead! We're dead!" While Violet says hysterically, "It blew up." Then Dash says, "We survived but we're dead!" Mrs. Incredible splashes ocean water at both of them and says, "We are not going to die. Now both of you will get a grip, or so help me I will ground you for a month. Understand!" This snaps the kids out of it.

I was devastated. It felt like freefall, despite the fact that I knew Lyme was curable; the fact that I had it almost drove me underwater. Why would God put this new challenge in front of me? He wanted to test me, but I didn't see that then. All I saw was a sickness that would haunt me for the rest of the year, and unannounced to me, for years to come.

Aside from the new sickness, my only two "close" friends were disgusted that I had changed my name. They denied every ounce of it. At first, I thought they were just in denial and they would get over it, but they didn't. Instead, the two grew more distant by the day, and started ignoring me. At least that's the way I saw it. They didn't see the changes that were taking place. They didn't see that I was going from a shy, insecure girl to a confidant young woman.

All they saw was a girl who was trying to turn into her favorite movie character. My two "friends" would have their own little secret conversations, but when talking to me the answers were always one word answers. It bugged me, and didn't help my depression any.

It was at this point that Kira and I became closer friends. I remember one day at church when I broke down and she took my hand, pulled me downstairs to the undercroft, sat me down and told me, "Talk." I told her the whole friendship situation, which I had been holding inside for quiet some time. Seeing how deeply hurt I was made her mad for what was happening. She offered for me to sit with her and her friends at lunch. I took her up on that offer after working up enough courage to leave the "comfort" of my old "friends."

Okay, so I didn't know at the time that I had depression or that I was even going down that road, but I had lost the will to smile, the will to laugh. Those who knew me well knew that I was always smiling, always giggling, if not laughing. But, by the end of the year 2010, no one could get me to do either. Now I had noticed the shift long before the end of the year, and had most certainly wondered why. I asked a friend who wasn't so "close", and her response to me was something like this, "Well, not everybody smiles all the time. It's natural. Perhaps you've just backed off, which isn't a bad thing at all." I would like to have believed her, but I couldn't help but think something wasn't quite right.

Chapter 14

One More
By Superchick

I have everything to lose. I'm not getting up to fight. I might get used to giving up so I am showing up tonight. I am my own enemy. The battle fought within my mind. If I can overcome step one, I can face the ninety – nine...

Battle of Depression

No, something wasn't right, and by the end of the year it was clear. My art teacher and Kira were the only two who could even make me muster a smile. More than once I had wanted to go to sleep and never wake up. I wanted to go home to Heaven to Father God. Yet, that wasn't what God wanted for me to do. My time on this planet wasn't done.

Reality became a harsh place for me and I was escaping more and more into my imagination.

My mind had become a bloody battlefield, and my imagination was just as dark as my thoughts. However, it seemed to help me cope. I was fighting, internally. There was someone, something, in my head, telling me one word thoughts, as if it were from another distant planet, underneath my scull, but away from my brain. I kept on telling this internal voice, "No!" I was a Super fighting; fighting a villain within my mind. I couldn't give up. I would never give up. But it was getting harder and harder for me to stay afloat. It was hard for me to just stay focused on schoolwork that I knew I needed to get done.

By February of 2011, I looked like a "walking zombie" to the outside world. I was not doing well at all. My feet finally took me to my guidance counselor, and, without any warning, I told her everything. Starting from having had Lyme disease, to my friendship dramas, to where I was, with the thoughts that haunted my head. I told it all, and at the end, I broke down.

Chapter 15

One Step at a Time
By Jorden Sparks

When you can't wait any longer. But there's no end in sight. It's the faith that makes you stronger. The only way we get there is one step at a time…

Fix it, Now!

That evening, I found myself back in the hospital. It turns out that the medication I was on, had, well, a side effect of depression! Now they tell us! My neurologist had decided I needed emergency admission to the hospital in order to quickly change my anti-seizure medication. Following the med change it felt like a huge weight was lifted off my head. So much relief! I spent five days in the hospital and then two weeks at home recovering. Truthfully, they, for once, "fixed it" and "fixed it" well. The following week was February vacation and we had made plans to go down to Florida for a college interview at Beacon College, and I so wasn't giving that up. All of us needed a break from the home stress.

In Sarasota, Florida, besides managing to take a tour of Ringling College of Art and Design, I met my soon-to-be prom date. He was such a gentleman and had a great sense of humor. The new improved me came out to shine once again. Suddenly, I had a date for senior prom. We seriously needed to get to know each other better. All in due time, I suppose.

By the time I came back to school it was my birthday and I had made plans with my amazing friend, Kira, to just hang out together after school. I had had enough of the drama and didn't exactly want to deal with it that day. Problem fixed. Drama gone.

Kira and I went to see a movie called Beastly, which was based off of Beauty and The Beast. The movie was wonderful! Afterwards we went out to eat, and then back to my house for dessert, and, of course, presents.

Weather on my birthday is always strange. You never know what to expect. However, this year's weather was particularly strange. It went from being a nice overcast evening, to rainy and windy, knocking out the power at my house. Woo–we, I got it all in one day!

So everything was fixed and all right. That is what I thought at least. Little did I know things were going to go for a landslide in the near future.

Chapter 16

Keep Holding On
By Avril Lavigne
When it gets cold and feels like the end. There's no place to go. You know I won't give in. No, I won't give in. Keep holding on, cause you know we'll make it through, we'll make it through. Just stay strong, 'cause you know I'm here for you, I'm here for you…

Now What?

Months came and went and soon I graduated from high school. Only days later, Kira adopted me as her little sister. We had become very, very, close and I accepted the new role as a special gift from her. I had never had any siblings and loved the opportunity to be chosen. But soon June had passed and July had come, bringing with it some new issues.

My seizure activity started up again and I was practically having auras every day and full blown seizures every two weeks. Great! Now what? It didn't lighten up, and my epilepsy had made itself known once again. Dad believed it was a co-infection from the Lyme. I didn't like to think that, and, the herbal medicine I was taking almost proved otherwise: A herxheimer reaction of a full blown seizure every other day from just one drop.

I continued doing neurofeedback, which helped some, but not enough, so I stopped at the end of July. When you're nineteen there is this urge that comes over you to be more independent. For most, that means going to college. This wasn't true for me, but I was going through the same independent struggle every teen goes through. The only difference was I couldn't escape. To be honest I made the decision to stop doing neurofeedback. **I Made the Decision**! And I didn't want to go back on it, no matter how hard people tried. I had been doing neurofeedback since 2003 and I was finally tired of it. I was tired of Dad "playing doctor." I was tired of taking a million (exaggerating here) things. I was tired of being sick. I was tired of people trying to "fix me." Doctors and friends of Dad's can say what they want to. They have a right to their opinion. However, no matter how hard they try to explain to me that nothing is "wrong with me", they're really saying it. I don't care what they think.

To make things seem even worse, my neurologist didn't want to put me on any new anti-seizure medication.

Now what? What could I do to make this better? Where was the light at the end of the tunnel? Where was the flicker of hope when I needed it the most?

Chapter 17

Beauty from Pain By Superchick
And though I can't understand why this happened, I know that I will when I look back some day, and see how you've brought beauty from ashes, and made me as gold purified through these flames. After all this has passed, I still will remain…

A Flicker of Hope

Well, God has a plan for me. He has His reasons for what He puts into my life. This was among them: The idea of a seizure alert dog came into play. A long time ago, I had wanted one, but didn't have enough seizures to qualify for one. Well, God brought it to my consciousness once again. Actually, my mom brought it into my mind. Now, by this time, I wasn't sure. I was skeptical and disbelieving. I emailed Mom three different links to assistant dog organizations that trained seizure alert dogs. I thought I didn't qualify for a dog in any of these organizations, and these links would prove my point. However,

I was wrong. Only moments later, I discovered that, in fact, I did qualify.

After some discussion with my parents, I applied to an organization, and waited for a response. There are many organizations out there, but this one seemed to be one of the best. When I didn't hear back after a month, I decided to contact them. When they realized that I hadn't heard from them, they thanked me for getting in touch, and told me that the trainers had reviewed my application and would like me to come down for an interview. After my questions were answered over the phone, an interview was scheduled and the process began.

There was now a flicker of hope in the air, the possibilities seemingly endless at this new idea. May this be the answer to my prayer.

Chapter 18

Lions!
By The Listening
Be steady on your feet no matter the trouble you meet. Lions make you brave. Giants give you faith. Death is a charade. You don't have to feel safe to feel unafraid…
I'm learning how to get up off my knees, and all it takes is practice…

Right to the Core

The interview at Canine Partners for Life went well, as everybody believed it would, but what bothered me was how scattered I felt. The question that stumped me was, "What would an ideal dog be for you?" Honestly, I had no clue how to answer. I had never had a dog and I had most certainly not grown up around them. The experiences I had around dogs were not the most favorable of memories. I had been quite literally run over by a golden retriever by the name of Taz when I was seven.

Therefore, I'll say it now, right to the core, I was scared. I had no idea how I was going to handle this, but I knew I was ready. I was still getting over my fear of dogs and this was a perfect opportunity for me to see how far I had come.

After the interview I got to meet a much bragged about dog named Forest. He was striking both in color and in personality. He was a sable colored, smooth coated collie. He was a very gentle and quiet dog. He said hello to each of us in his unique way, but gravitated towards me. He sniffed me as if asking, "Who are you? Something about you is different." I felt comfortable enough to pet him at permission from the volunteer walking him. He was already matched to another recipient. I would obviously not be receiving him, and it was a bit disappointing. Dad believed he and I would have made a good match and even he said, "If I had to choose any dog here, I would take him home in a heart beat." Coming from my dad, that's saying a lot.

From that experience, I realized I had come far. God already knew I had come far, and He just wanted to show me how far I had come. He also knows how far I will continue to grow in this area. At this time, I was also beginning to have a new outlook on my epilepsy: A realization that God really does have a plan, that epilepsy really was a gift from Him. A new beginning was around the corner and He would put new friends in my path to help guide me along.

Chapter 19

> ### We R Who We R
> ### By Ke$ha
>
> Hot and dangerous. If you're one of us, then roll with us...
>
> And, no, you don't wanta mess with us, got Jesus on my necklace-s-s...

A New Friend

The next step forward was to go back down there to Pennsylvania for two team training sessions or one graduate support class in order to qualify for the waiting list. We didn't want to leave the organization hanging, so we opted for two team training sessions, the first of which was scheduled to begin in about two weeks. Almost immediately we were on the road again.

So the unexpected happens sometimes. It's, to my way of thinking, called "God's Time" and, well, God's Time was mixed in this trip with Human's Time. It turns out that in the process of going down to attend these team training sessions, I met a new friend.

Figure 4 - Making new friends

Her name is Ruby and she was training with her recently acquired service dog, Sugar. They make quite a pair. She and I could relate on a level that many other people could not. In fact, all of the recipients here, with their recently matched new companions, could relate on a similar level. We've all been through the ringer. We've all faced the impossible, and, with God's help, we have prevailed, and are still prevailing.

Figure 5 - Ruby and Sugar with Me and Alex (l-r)

Like me, Ruby has a seizure disorder. She also had many other challenges complicating that one. Things were rocky for her, like they seemed to be for me. The differences seemed to blend into the background while the similarities were too great to be ignored.

Basically, we hit it off right away, with her one step ahead of me, and a few states apart. Our friendship hung in the balance. It has not crumbled or fallen, but has faded amongst the fog of life. A new friend, a new test.

Every now and then I receive an email from her saying how well she is doing. Sugar has given Ruby a great deal of independence and the terrific duo are now off at college making new friends. Hearing about her successes with Sugar by her side, really makes me wonder, "Who will **my** service dog be?"

Chapter 20

We Three Kings
By Anne Murray
Oh , oh, oh, star of wonder, star of night. Star of royal beauty bright. Westward leading, still proceeding, guide us to thy perfect light...

One Wish

At the end of my visit to Canine Partners for Life, I got a chance to meet one of the puppies who was in training, and that I had seen on Facebook only two days after I came back from my interview. Her name is Lira. She's the sweetest dog I've ever met. At only five months old she is already quick to calm down and quiet, no matter the interaction. She has a gorgeous face and, though I knew I was setting myself up for this, I quickly bonded with her. AAAAHHHH! I knew it would happen, I just knew it would, but God has His reasons, right? So He must have His reasons for this.

Wanting a service dog is not just a wish, but rather a need. Wanting a particular service dog is a wish and only a wish. You can hope, you can pray, but there is never any guarantee that the particular dog you want will be the one you get.

The organization I've applied to does not go based on who has the most need, but rather what are the dog's needs and what are yours. Making the best match possible is the goal!

I understand all that, and I get it. It makes sense. But if I could have only one wish, that wish would be for Lira to be the one; the one I would rely on to alert me to an oncoming seizure, the one who will help me get my independence back, the one who, with God's help, will save my life.

She's the dog I want, the only true-to-my-heart gift I'm wishing for Christmas this year. While I know she won't come to me on Christmas Day, she will still be my one wish, my one Christmas wish.

Chapter 21

> While I'm Waiting
> By John Waller
> ___
> I'm waiting on you Lord. Though it's not easy, no, but faithfully I will wait…

How Long

In terms of anything I can do to get my service dog, waiting is now all that's left and it's pretty difficult. I myself was even more anxious at the beginning, but I have since calmed down.

The distractions of writing this story, reading good books, and creating art pieces help. I'll admit I'm not in the best of shape, but the thought of Lira keeps me going.

It's the thought of Lira, the hope that the dog will actually be her, which keeps me from becoming an emotional wreck. I just can picture the two of us doing so many things together. I think she and I would be great for each other, but I can only hope. She needs to be able to alert and that's not determined yet. So it's all in God's hands now. I just have to remind myself to "let go and let God." That's the best thing to do, as much as I wish things could move faster. Hey! What did I just say? Oh, sorry Lira. Let me clarify…things are moving as fast as they can. Lira hasn't completed her training yet. The dogs have to be two years of age, or a year and nine months before they can be matched. I'm just way too excited.

What gets me is, I have no control at all as to when I will get the service dog or which one it will be. None! How long will it take? How long will I have to wait? Well, that's all in God's Time isn't it? Yes. God shows us things in the right moment and time. He waits for us to be ready. So I'll just have to be patient and see what He shows me.

Chapter 22

True Colors
By –M.Y.M.P.
True colors are shining through. And I see your true colors and that's why I love you. So don't be afraid to let them show…

Miracle

God works miracles in the most amazing ways and most often when were not expecting them. He has certainly worked a number of them in my life and this one was no exception. I got a call on the sixteenth of April, 2012, from Canine Partners for Life saying they had a match! Can you guess who? It was Forest! Can you believe it? I know I can't. It's hard to believe, really. I mean, no one would have thought that I might actually end up with him.

Figure 6 - Forest!

It turns out that the first match didn't work out, so he was back and ready to be matched again. Now that was truly God's hand at work. I mean, seriously, there is no other way I could have gotten matched with Forest.

I realized, as much as I had been wishing for Lira, Forest had been my first pick. As I said to Mom, Lira might have been a wish, but Forest was a dream. I hadn't given much thought to it, because he had been matched with someone else back in the fall, but if he hadn't been, I'm sure I would have been wishing for him. He's just that kind of dog.

I was so excited after getting over the shock and breathlessness of it all. I couldn't get over it that day. I was so happy that it was Forest. Whether he picked me out that day we first met or not; I don't know. I wouldn't be surprised if he did. I believe he saw my true colors and I saw his.

I had been at my lowest low since my firm diagnoses of Lyme disease back in January. This exciting news, this miracle, lifted my spirits high above the clouds. I felt like I was flying! Well, almost.

The more I thought about Forest, the more I loved him, that beautiful sable colored collie whose calm and gentle manner makes him so approachable. He's just my kind of dog, or so I believe. I guess I'll find out how true that belief is when I go to team training. I'm just so excited! But, first things first, I have to prepare: mentally, physically, and financially.

Chapter 23

> ### Help Me Out God
> ### By Superchick
>
> Help me out God, I need a little something. Just enough so I don't lose hope before morning. Because in the sun things will work out just fine, cause the night's been extra long, I fear I won't make it to the dawn because the night is dark and I might doubt. And I might doubt because I can't hope without you, God. I can't hope without you, God...

Today

As time passes by, my auras get worse. Light sensitivity is a huge problem, if you want to look at it that way. I'm wearing sunglasses most of the time, except, of course, for at home.

I'm continuing to battle the Lyme disease, which is just emphasizing my neurological symptoms and sensitivities, making everything worse. Even though I had completed a three month course of oral antibiotics over a year ago, a recent antibiotic challenge urine test, known as the Multiplex PCR test, showed I definitely still have Lyme. Once again, I am on some heavy-duty oral antibiotics and I am now experiencing some really severe nausea. It has been an emotional roller coaster from the start, one moment something will tip me off, while the next moment I'll be ecstatic.

Friends are important to me. They mean a lot. They can and always have helped me through the toughest of times, and I've helped them. However, with all my friends at college across the states, our friendships have been stretched, and I'm feeling the effects. As always, being sick has its downside, and, because of it, I have not made any new friends who are close by. However, two exceptions to this are a friend I made over Deviant Art, an artist website where artists come together from across the world, and a friend I made at a Lyme Support group.

Today I am looking forward to meeting my new furry companion, and yet I need some help. God is always helping me, but I also need some help from some very special people. Those people are all of you, those willing to donate and sponsor my cause. The fact that you have bought this book, and are reading it, has already helped. Thank you.

Naturally, a service dog isn't free of charge. The total cost of training and placing a service dog is about $24,000. I only have to donate a fraction of that amount, but, still, it's large enough. The donation I have to make is about $1,200. How long it will take to get the money for this is ever so unclear. Everything is unclear when it comes to cost. Especially since the donation isn't the only thing I have to worry about. I also have to consider the cost of the upcoming trip to Pennsylvania for three weeks of training and what it will cost for the maintenance of the dog. Not including the donation, the approximate total cost for the round-trip and initial dog supplies, I estimate to be in the neighborhood of $4,000, depending on how fortunate we are with regard to accommodations.

God has helped me get this far and will continue to help me every day. He knows the future and I do not. God knows what's in store for me and will show me at the right time. He always has, and I believe He will put the right people in my life who are willing to help me now.

Future donations and money I receive from selling copies of this book will go towards helping my furry friend stay happy and healthy. So, please, don't feel shy, don't think I've completed my mission even when I've come back from the three week training course. I haven't. Canine Partners for Life is an organization that binds you, becomes part of your life, and an extension of your family. Forest and I will continue to make trips down to Canine Partners for Life to freshen-up on our skills. Forest will also need regular trips to the vet to keep him in good health and tick free.

Right now, I'm just waiting to spread my wings and fly. With help from God and you, I will. I'm longing to become independent and fly from the nest, but without some help, the task is nearly impossible. So please, join me today, because today makes the difference of a lifetime.

For additional
donations, please make
them payable to Corey
Snook, I.T.F. Violet
Snook, and send to:

Corey Snook
MBTI
PO Box 754
Meredith, NH 03253

Epilogue

Colors that complement stand out in such magnificent ways. Abstraction is only one form that they can take. Let the music make the lines and designs that come from the artist's hand. Behind the artist's eyes there is always something new, something delightful, and something surprising. The artist is a creator: she has created and painted her past. She sheds color on the shades of gray, the unknown lines and mysterious designs. She cannot control what her hand paints or what her eyes see, but she can say what she believes, what is her own and what has been given to her by her Father, Master Creator of all. The wings she seeks are so far away, impossibly challenging to receive, and yet, she still keeps painting, painting to the beat. Thanks for joining her as she relives her path, up to the present point, and continues to find the courage within the artist's hand, to unfold.

The courage within the artist's hand is something that many seek. For how bold can the artist's hand be? The artist's hand holds the brush and helps it make the strokes and designs, the curves and the lines that you see. The courage is within the artist's hand because, without the hand, a thought, an idea, is just that and nothing more. Without the hand, an artist's idea would not become an artist's creation, and a masterpiece would not be born.

Acknowledgements

A teacher so special to me, a leader so great, leading a Girl Scout team, she silently led me right into writing. She encouraged me all the way through. She helped me complete my first story, which inspired me to go on to the next step. A goal was set. An ambition was made. That one little push, back in sixth grade, got me here, where I am today, publishing my first book.

Thank you, Lucy Gustafson Chaplin, for all your support and encouragement.

I also acknowledge a wise and patient neurologist with an amazing memory, who saw me through many long years, gently guiding my family through the ups and the downs of this ever winding road, showering us with advice and knowledge along the way. You stood by us as we tried neurofeedback. Thank you, Dr. James Riviello, for all your guidance and understanding.

To my editors: good friend Dottie Craft, my mother Connie Snook, my father Corey Snook, and my teacher Lucy Gustafson Chaplin who all helped make this book possible to publish. Thank you so very much!

Citations

1. Rambach, Rachel. "German Cradle Song." MP3. Songs for Teaching. March 1, 2012. http://www.songsforteaching.com/lullabies/germancradlesong.php

2. Winchell, Paul, Songwriter: Sherman, Richard M. Sherman, Robert B. "Tigger's Song." The Page at Pooh Corner. March 1, 2012. 2005. http://www.pooh-corner.org/tigger_lyrics.shtml

3. Denver, John. "Potter's Wheel." The Best of John Denver. CD. Delta Music Co. 2004.

4. Relient K, Songwriter: Thiessen, Matthew Arnold. "More Than Useless." Miscellaneous. Flv. SongLyrics. March 1, 2012. 2012. http://www.songlyrics.com/relient-k/more-than-useless-lyrics/

5. Collins, Phil, Songwriters: Mancina, Mark & Collins, Phil. "On My Way" Brother Bear. CD. Walt Disney Records. 2009.

6. Brake, Karen. "Believe in Myself." MP3. Triple Threat Sonic Heroes Vocal Trax. Sonic Retro. May 1, 2012. http://info.sonicretro.org/index.php?title=Triple_Threat_Sonic_Heroes_Vocal_Trax&diff=104423&oldid=104422

7. McCartney, Jesse. "Daddy's Little Girl." Right Where You Want Me. CD. Hollywood Records. 2006.

8. Clarkson, Kelly. "Breakaway." Kelly Clarkson Breakaway. CD. Phantom Sound and Vision. 2009.

9. Within Temptation. "Angels." The Silent Force. CD. Roadrunner Records. 2005.

10. Alabama. "I'm in a Hurry (and Don't Know Why)." Ultimate Alabama 20 #1 Hits. CD. RCA. 2004.

11. Harris, Krystal. "Supergirl." The Princess Diaries (Original Soundtrack). CD. Walt Disney Records. 2001.

12. Superchick. "Stand in the Rain." Rock What You've Got. CD. Inpop Records. 2008.

13. Digby, Marie. "Miss Invisible." Unfold. MP3. Hollywood Records, Inc. 2008.

14. Superchick. "One More." Rock What You Got. CD. Impop Records. 2008.

15. Sparks, Jorden. "One Step at a Time." Jorden Sparks. MP3. Zomba Recording LLC. 2007.

16. Lavigne, Avril. "Keep Holding On." The Best Damn Thing. MP3. RCA Records, a Unit of SONEY BMG Music Entertainment. 2007.

17. Superchick. "Beauty From Pain." Beauty From Pain I.L. CD. Impop Records. 2006.

18. The Listening. "Lions!" Lights. MP3. Sire Records for the U.S. and WEA International Inc. 2009.

19. Ke$ha. "We R Who We R." We R Who We R. CD. 101 Distribution. 2010.

20. Murray, Anne. "We Three Kings." What a Wonderful Christmas. CD. Straightway. 2001.

21. Waller, John. "While I'm Waiting." While I'm Waiting. CD. Reunion. 2009.

22. M.y.m.p. "True Colors." Flv. YouTube. May 1, 2012. http://www.youtube.com/watch?v=I0vE2ZElogU

23. Superchick. "Help Me Out God." Karaoke Superstars. CD. Inpop Records. 2002.

About the Author

Violet grew up in the beautiful, small town of Meredith, New Hampshire. She has some wonderful insight into her past and has always had a little wisdom to offer. Having her own share of ups and downs, she understands what it is like to be different, and yet she keeps moving forward every step of the way. With a unique past and inspiring courage, this young woman is truly a Super at heart.

"My family, my friends, and Canine Partners for Life, have shown me that when it feels like the end, and you're in the dark, a candle is lit, a light has been turned on, and you can see again," says Violet.